SUCCESS IN GROUPWORK

POCKET STUDY SKILLS

Peter Hartley & Mark Dawson

palgrave
macmillan

First published 2010 by
PALGRAVE MACMILLAN

Palgrave Macmillan in the UK is an imprint of Macmillan Publishers Limited, registered in England, company number 785998, of Houndmills, Basingstoke, Hampshire RG21 6XS.

Palgrave Macmillan in the US is a division of St Martin's Press LLC, 175 Fifth Avenue, New York, NY 10010.

Palgrave Macmillan is the global academic imprint of the above companies and has companies and representatives throughout the world.

Palgrave® and Macmillan® are registered trademarks in the United States, the United Kingdom, Europe and other countries

ISBN-13: 978-0-230-27230-9

This book is printed on paper suitable for recycling and made from fully managed and sustained forest sources. Logging, pulping and manufacturing processes are expected to conform to the environmental regulations of the country of origin.

A catalogue record for this book is available from the British Library.

A catalog record for this book is available from the Library of Congress.

10 9 8 7 6 5
19 18 17 16 15

Printed in China

Contents

Acknowledgements

This book was inspired by our involvement in the LearnHigher CETL. Our thanks go to all involved for their encouragement and support, with particular thanks to our current partners in the 'Making Groupwork Work' resource – Carol Elston and Julia Braham from the University of Leeds and Tony Lowe from Webducate.

Thanks must go to our series editor, Kate Williams, for her tireless commitment to plain language, and to Suzannah Burywood and colleagues at Palgrave Macmillan for their support and patience. We have learned a lot from this experience.

A final thanks to all the student groups we have worked with, especially the ones who delivered outcomes and presentations way beyond our expectations. Hopefully, this book will inspire many more to do the same.

Introduction

Most courses in higher education ask students to work in groups and/or include an assessed group project where your grade will depend on the way your group has worked together. How are you going to make the most of this experience?

Your tutors may expect you just to 'get on with it' and not give you much guidance on how to organise yourselves. Even if the tutors do provide support and sessions on groupwork, they cannot be available all the time. But this book can!

We use examples of real student groups who made their groupwork successful, including:

- the engineering students who discovered a lifetime interest in their first meeting (see p. 27)
- the business students who worked out how to play the business game and learned much more than their tutors expected (p. 96)
- the design students who could not agree but managed to find a winning compromise (p. 88)
- the media students who took a risk by 'reversing' the task and impressing the tutor (p. 40)

▶ the social science students who forgot to argue (p. 104).

As these examples illustrate, there is no one best way of organising your group. You have to think about and adapt our ideas and suggestions to your own situation. But this will help you become more effective and that is what good learning is all about.

Using this guide

This book is divided into five parts that cover key aspects of groupwork:

Part 1: Getting ready for groupwork – is about understanding why groups are used and what you can get out of them.

Part 2: Creating the team – looks at how you can set up the first few meetings to make a positive start.

Part 3: Organising your group – suggests ways of planning and organising your-selves to make the best use of your time and skills.

Part 4: Relationships and communication – suggests ways of thinking about the group as a whole, effective ways of communicating and managing the relationships in the group, and what to do if things go wrong.

Part 5: Assessment and reflection – suggests ways of reviewing your group experience, writing this up for assessment, and action planning for your future practice.

Each part ends with 'takeaway tips' to summarise the most important ideas.

This book focuses on the most demanding test of your group skills – where you are put in a small group and given a major assessed task which will take you several weeks, a semester or even a year to complete. But you can apply all the ideas in this book to more limited examples of groupwork. For example, if you are asked to work in a short discussion group in a class session it is worth spending a few minutes checking the task (see p. 34) and working out who the other group members are (see p. 25).

Assignments and reflection

Group projects will ask you to produce a 'product'. This will depend on the sort of course you are on – it may be something physical like a design or piece of software or it may be some kind of report or theoretical argument. You may have to present your conclusions to an audience of tutors or other students. We offer suggestions on presentations in pp. 92–4.

Many group projects will ask you to reflect on your group experience in a written assignment. At key points, we include relevant **theory boxes** and then suggest short reflective exercises that will help you write up your experience for assessment. This is an increasingly common part of the assessment of group projects and we say more about this on pp. 97–101. These opportunities to reflect are indicated by the **Hmm ...** logo. Combining your reflections with further investigation of theory will give you a very solid basis for any reflective assignment.

About the authors

Between us, we have worked with a wide range of student groups, from designing and delivering courses based on group projects to advising students on how best to approach collaboration. We are members of the team behind 'Making Groupwork Work', the online resource (at www.learnhighergroupwork.com/) which analyses video clips of a student group working through a group project and offers suggestions and links to a wide range of helpful materials.

Taking it further

Finally, we have developed webpages to support this book. These contain further examples/updates and you can download all the documents and checklists we have recommended (www.palgrave.com/pocketskills/groupwork).

PART 1

GETTING READY FOR GROUPWORK

This part is about understanding why groups are used in higher education and what you can get out of them. We recommend reading it before you start working in your group. It will explain:

▶ why students work in groups at university
▶ what you can expect from groupwork
▶ what the key challenges of groupwork are.

Three reasons are usually given:

1 It makes efficient use of resources.
2 It develops valuable skills for your future career.
3 It provides a richer, 'deep-learning' experience.

Resources

More students attend university than ever before, increasing demands on resources which have not expanded at the same rate. Groupwork allows resources, such as library material and room facilities, to be shared. There is also the assessment load on tutors – 40 group reports or presentations are much quicker to mark than 200 individual assignments.

Developing valuable skills

Most job descriptions include a 'person specification' which describes the skills and qualities they are looking for in individuals who will do the job well. This list includes skills which are seen as important in virtually all organisations (key skills) and skills which can be used across a range of different situations (transferable skills). One of these skills is usually groupwork/teamwork.

Universities encourage activities to help students develop skills such as 'working with other people' because it is clear that this is what employers are looking for. As a student, group projects mean opportunities to develop valuable skills for your future career.

You will be asked questions about your experience of working with others in job or career interviews. Think about yourself from the perspective of a future employer: how many questions from the checklist on the next page can you answer now?

Groupwork checklist for job interviews

	Your answer
What sort of experience have you had in groups?	
How do you typically behave in groups? What is your major contribution to a group?	
What have you learned from your experience?	
How did you help the groups you worked in to sort out any difficulties or conflict?	
What examples and evidence can you show to convince future employers that you have the skills and understanding to work in groups in their context?	

Don't worry if you weren't able to give answers to all the questions! This book is designed to point you to the skills you can gain through groupwork, so that you *will* be able to answer them.

Learning experience

Research into how people learn has come up with a number of theories over the years that have been influential in universities and other organisations involved in teaching. Students often report that they learn more from working on a project with other people than they do from individual assignments. In short, they often report a 'deeper' or 'richer' learning experience.

Theory box: Learning through experience

Theory

In the 1970s, David Kolb proposed a theory of 'Experiential Learning' which describes learning as a cyclical process with four key stages: experience; observation; conceptualisation; and experimentation (Kolb 1984).

Experiential learning has been hugely influential in modern education practice and can be seen today in the widespread use of approaches like problem-based learning, reflective practice and small-group activity.

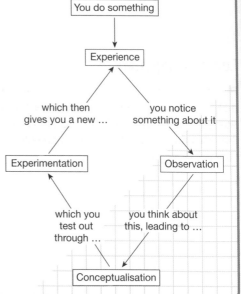

Comment

As with any model in the social sciences, Kolb's ideas have been investigated and tested by other academics and practitioners. Some have offered criticisms that:

- learning often occurs without clearly adhering to the four-stage cycle
- Kolb gives little attention to the role of learner motivation and goals in the process
- the importance of reflection is understated
- the model does not take into account the complexity and variety of modern learners.

How can you use Kolb's model to help develop your understanding of groups?

- What do you look out for when you are working in a group?
- Do you make time to reflect on what is happening?
- Do you try to make sense of what is going on in order to do things differently and achieve more in the future?

Any other thoughts?

You are sitting in the first class of the module. The tutor is going through what to expect during this module. You hear the following words: '… and you will be working in groups from week three'.

What are your initial reactions? Which thought bubbles are closest to your reaction?

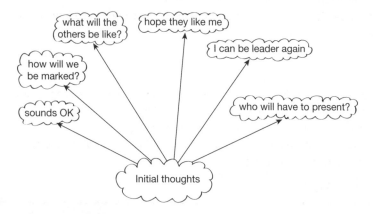

Most students have mixed expectations about working in a group. On the positive side, you can look forward to developing new relationships and achieving more than you could on your own. On the negative side, you may be worried about whether the members will get along or whether you will be able to develop a really positive team spirit.

There is no one best way of organising your group. You have to think about and adapt our ideas and suggestions to your own situation.

Looking beyond your immediate group

For many students, the thought of working with other people can seem a bit scary. However, great achievements often come from teams – they can usually achieve bigger and better things. Everywhere you look there are companies, organisations, service teams – people working together to get stuff done which they could not do on their own.

Many start-up companies and social enterprises came from a small group (often of students) who spotted an opportunity and decided to run with it – Google, for example.

Working effectively with other people takes a bit of getting used to. It is a valuable skill and, like any skill, you get better at it with practice.

The main challenges that students face when working on group projects tend to fall into one of three main categories: communication, organisation and workload.

Communication and relationships

Group members have to get along with each other (you do not have to like everybody, though) and keep each other informed about important developments.

Effective communication doesn't just mean that people understand you. You also need to understand everybody and each group member needs to feel confident that their thoughts will be listened to and considered fairly. Many problems faced by groups are a result of poor (or complete lack of) communication.

Organisation

Groups have to organise themselves, and plan how to manage their time and their project.

Often groups run into difficulties because they have not organised sufficiently to have a grip on who is supposed to be doing what and by when.

Workload

Group members have to agree to (and complete) a fair share of the workload. One of the most common complaints from students about groupwork is that some group members are not participating or contributing enough to the project.

At the very least, these three common issues can cause inconvenience and might result in more stress and a less successful project. At worst, a complete breakdown in communication and work progress could result in a failed project.

Most of the detailed suggestions in this book relate to one or more of these issues, so it is worth regularly going back to the fundamental questions. Try using a simple checklist approach to monitor how you are doing.

Key issues checklist

	Check box ✓	Evidence/examples (remember you may need to write this up for an assignment)
Are we communicating effectively?		
Are we well organised?		
Are we sharing the workload?		

Theory box: What makes groups successful?

Theory

Social scientists have identified several important characteristics which influence team performance. These include:

- a common purpose
- group members' commitment to the group goals
- group members' motivations and abilities
- having a mix of expertise and backgrounds in the group (Seethamraju and Borman 2009).

These characteristics are also identified in many of the guides or handbooks for managers. For example, the Harvard Business School guide, *Teams That Click* (2004), suggests 'three essentials of an effective team': commitment, competence and a common goal.

Comment

Most of this work has looked at groups in organisations where there is an established hierarchy and status structure, and where there is almost inevitably a 'boss' who is held formally responsible for the group. This is not the norm in student groups where the group has to work out its own structure. So you cannot automatically generalise from organisational groups to student groups. Research on student groups has not been as comprehensive, so do test out the theory against your own experience.

In your experience of working in groups, what have been the most important characteristics?

▶ How do they relate to the characteristics identified by social scientists?
▶ Can you compare the experience of working in a group with a boss and working in a group without one?

∘ ○ ∘

Takeaway tips

- Before you start to work in a new group, think about what you can gain from it, both in terms of a learning experience and in terms of how it could help your future career – how can you use and reflect on the experience to talk to a future employer?
- Consider your expectations about groupwork – how will they influence your behaviour?
- Do you have ideas on how groups can best manage the challenges we have identified?
- See if you can find some research on groups in your subject area – can you pick up any useful tips?

PART 2 CREATING THE TEAM

This part examines ways to make sure that the group starts out as an effective working team. It looks at:

▶ how groups are selected
▶ how to get the first meeting right
▶ how to agree your ground rules.

Tutors can use one of three ways:

1 Random allocation (like counting off people where they are sitting 1, 2, 3, ... 6).
2 Letting students choose themselves.
3 Tutor allocation – where the tutor uses some preset criteria to form the groups.

Each method has advantages and disadvantages, and may lead you to a different approach in your first meeting.

Random allocation

If your group has been chosen randomly then the mix of abilities and temperaments will also be random. This can be useful. For example, the group will usually generate a wide variety of different ideas. On the other hand, there is a higher risk of conflict due to personal differences. One practical consequence is that you should spend enough time getting to know the other members and making sure that you identify all the skills that different individuals bring to the group.

Choosing your own group

This sounds attractive, but there are possible pitfalls. If you simply choose your friends, they may not be the best combination of people for the task. Your friends are likely to be similar to you in their outlook and attitudes – this may mean that only a limited range of opinions are expressed. On the other hand, working with people you know means you are more likely to already have some knowledge of their strengths and weaknesses. This can help the group get started more quickly.

In this situation you should think carefully about how you choose the other members of your group. Which combination of your friends is most likely to demonstrate the characteristics of successful groups (see theory box on p. 13)?

Tutor allocation

The tutor may allocate students to groups to achieve a mix, taking into account learning styles, cultural backgrounds or other criteria. However your group has been selected, thinking about how it was selected and the effects of this method can give you useful points for reflection.

Theory box: How should groups be selected?

Theory

Organisations are paying more attention to the way they put working groups together to make sure that the group has the right mix of social and technical skills. They may use evidence and techniques from social science such as the role analysis discussed in pages 47–55. There is growing research evidence that some characteristics of groups are very important. For example, Wheelan (2009) found that workgroups with three to six members were both more productive and more developed (see pp. 102–3) than groups with seven or more.

One recent study demonstrated that self-selected student groups were more likely to perform better if their members had taken account of factors like individual skills and knowledge, ability to manage tasks, and likely social cohesion, when they formed (Seethamraju and Borman 2009).

Comment

More research on student groups is needed so that we know which findings can be generalised, especially as other research has found major differences between different types of team (Chiocchio and Essiembre 2009). You should treat the outcomes of all social science research in this area as results which may only apply in specific circumstances and look for the similarities and differences with your experience.

How has your group been selected?

- What might be an advantage for your group?
- What might be a disadvantage?
- What does this mean for how you are going to operate?

∘ O ∘

5   The first meeting – getting it right

Making a positive start

The first time a student group meets together is very important. In many groups it will be the first time that you have met at least some of the other people in the group. Even if you know the other people, it may be the first time you have worked on the same project. In either case, the first meeting is where you get to know other group members and start organising the rest of the project. Getting it right can give you a big push on the way to success.

Be positive

Approach the meeting with a positive mindset, open to the idea of working with other people, or you run the risk of appearing negative to others. First impressions are important.

Positive people will encourage discussion and cooperation. How do you tend to react in a new group situation?

Behaviours that appear positive	Behaviours that can appear negative
Smiling	Frowning or looking bored
Facing the group	Not facing the group
Asking questions	Saying very little or nothing
Offering suggestions	Criticising others' ideas
Taking relevant notes	Focusing on technology (checking your mobile phone, laptop etc.)
Talking mostly about the project	Talking mostly about personal interests and non-project stuff

Think about what you might get out of the group project:

▶ What general skills might you learn?
▶ What might you learn about the subject?
▶ What might you learn about working with others?
▶ What might you learn about yourself?

∘ ○ ∘

Meeting places

Your first meeting may have to be held in the teaching room you are in, and a tiered lecture theatre makes it difficult, but do make the effort to move or turn your chairs around – so you are talking in a group, not sitting in a row!

When you meet outside teaching time, choose a place that *everyone* finds comfortable.

Setting the scene checklist

Does the location help you work together?	Check ✓
Can the group see each other clearly, preferably facing each other?	
Can you hear each other OK?	
If you need to share something or all look at something, can you do it easily without excluding anyone?	

Getting to know people

You need to find a conversation starter which helps you exchange information and which members of the group will not find intrusive or embarrassing.

Possible starting points include:

- How did you get on this course/module?
- Have you got previous experience of groupwork?
- What have we got in common?

Hmm...

How might you introduce yourself to a group for the first time?

- Is there something you could use to identify yourself uniquely?
- What are your likes/dislikes about groupwork?
- What are your strengths/weaknesses?

° O °

Examples

Business and Management group: Their task was to present for 10 minutes on what they had learnt over the semester about either interpersonal or intrapersonal skills for 30% of the overall module mark.

The group of eight had been allocated randomly and none knew each other well. They were told to sit together in order to get to know each other better, so they moved so they could sit in a circle. As they included students from the UK, from Eastern Europe and from China, they introduced themselves by explaining how to pronounce their names and comparing study styles for each of their countries.

Engineering group: In the first session of a major first-year module, each small group was given the task of finding out what they had in common. One group discovered that they all shared a passion for a particular brand of motorbike and became a very strong and cohesive group who supported each other for the duration of the three-year course.

Taking time

You may not instantly like all the other members of the group. This is another reason for taking time to get to know the other members. You may also want to reflect upon where your negative impressions have come from.

Can you think of a time when at first you weren't sure about someone but you grew to quite like them?

- Why were you not sure at first?
- What won you over?
- How might being mindful of this affect how you approach groupwork?

° O °

6 Agree your ground rules

A good way to get your group off to a good start is to agree guidelines or 'ground rules' to ensure that everyone is clear from the start about what is expected.

Ground rules can be divided roughly into two categories:

1 Communication and attitudes: how group members behave toward one another.
2 Working practice: group procedures and organisation.

Students' first thoughts about ground rules tend to focus on general aspects of communication, such as:

▶ treating everyone with respect and dignity

▶ giving people an opportunity to voice their ideas and opinions

▶ keeping others informed of anything that might affect the project (personal issues, for example)

▶ being professional and responsible.

Expressed like this, 'rules' do not necessarily translate easily into specific behaviour – for example, what do you understand by 'respect'? So try to give examples of how you want the group to behave and use something like the suggestions below to record your responses.

Example ground rules for communication and attitudes

Agreed principle	How we are going to do this
Treating everyone with respect and dignity	Use positive body language Give everyone a chance to speak Be polite to one another Listen and pay attention to each other Acknowledge other members' opinions

Example ground rules for working practice

Area of practice	What we agreed
When and where will the team meet?	Regular weekly meeting after the lecture.
Behave professionally	Turn up on time for meetings. No one should be more than 10 minutes late without sending a message to the rest of the group.

Area of practice	What we agreed
Will there be team or meeting roles?	Need to have someone take notes at each meeting. Everyone takes a turn at this.
How will we decide things?	Aim for consensus and only use voting as a last resort.

Other useful areas for ground rules include: how you are going to allocate work; what happens if someone is ill; what happens if someone doesn't do what they said they would.

Make sure one person writes up what you have agreed and emails it to everyone so there can be no vagueness about what was said. Review your ground rules from time to time to make sure they are working as you intended (see p. 74). If they are not, make changes – and again, make sure that you write down and circulate a single agreed version. Consider sending a copy to your tutor and discussing it with them if there is any tutorial time.

And so to the task

Do not forget the task – what the group has been asked to do or achieve. At the first meeting, make sure you share your understanding of what the task involves and start to plan what needs to be done.

You need to beware of rushing into detailed planning before you are sure that everybody agrees on what the group priorities are. And you need to deal with any anxieties from members who 'just want to get on with it'. Their ideas may not be shared by other members and may not be the most effective approach.

Part 3 of this book considers different ways of interpreting the task and planning actions.

Takeaway tips

- Adopt a positive attitude to the group experience.
- Get to know as much as you can about your team.
- Behave in ways which create and support a positive team environment.
- Set specific ground rules at the start (and don't forget to review them later).
- Get everyone's contact details!
- Agree a time/date and some initial actions for the next meeting.

PART 3 ORGANISING YOUR GROUP

This part suggests ways of organising your group to make the most effective use of your time. It includes the following issues:

- understanding the task
- considering team roles
- organising meetings
- making decisions.

7 Understanding the task

People often interpret instructions and tasks in different ways. So do not leap into specific activities before you are confident that all the group members share a common view of what you are trying to achieve.

Think about how you might approach the following three tasks before you read our analysis. What are the most important things you need to decide and prepare for?

Task A – for first-year Computing students

Select one of these topics: *Website development* or *Databases* or *Networking*. Present a poster that highlights latest developments in that area. Produce an accompanying fact sheet (not more than one side of A4).

Task B – for second-year Psychology students

Pupils in a class at a local secondary school are anxious about public speaking and presentations. Give them a 15-minute presentation on how to combat nerves, based on relevant psychological research and theory.

Study water pollution along the course of Bradford Beck. Write up your research as a scientific report for the council's Environmental Health Department and deliver a 20-minute presentation to members of the local council.

What do you have to do?

Look at the tutor's instructions very carefully. Make sure that you agree on what is required (and by when). Make sure you have details of all the practical requirements (e.g. deadlines, time for any presentation, rules on format etc.).

In the three examples above, there are very important differences between the tasks. For example:

- Different formats have different rules. There are specific rules and conventions for scientific reports but not always for posters or presentations.
- Your audiences are very different. In B and C, the tutors are taking on roles. In C, you might have to present to a real council member.
- The research is very different. In C you may have to do some practical work; in A and B, you need to go to published sources. In all three, you have to decide which research or information is most relevant.

You may not find all the information you need in the assignment brief:

▶ Tutors sometimes make mistakes and forget to include details that are important.
▶ Tutors may deliberately leave things open so that you have freedom of choice. For example, if you only have a time limit for a presentation then that may be because the tutor wants *you* to decide on the best presentation format (see pp. 92–5).

To make sure you have covered everything, take the tutor's instructions and rephrase them in your own words. Use the table below to record this and make sure everyone has a copy. When you have more experience of presentations in your subject, you might want to tailor this table to your context.

Understanding the assignment checklist

Key question	Your response
What do you think the project is about?	
What is the tutor expecting you to do?	

Key question	Your response
What does the assessment involve? Different methods make different demands on you and you need to decide what they involve and how to prepare for them, e.g. will there be any peer and self-assessment?	
What are the assessment criteria? How will the tutor distribute marks, e.g. will there be separate marks for content, format, presentation?	
What will the tutor think is a 'good' project? Look at the assessment criteria for the top marks to work out the key qualities.	
What sort of 'audience' will the tutors be when they receive your presentation and grade your assignment? For example, will they be acting as experts or will they be trying to judge how you can communicate to a non-expert audience?	

Example assignment checklist for Task A

Key question	Your response
What do you think the project is about?	We need to decide important developments in website design.
What is the tutor expecting you to do?	Library and internet research: make sure we cover the latest trade journals. We can earn extra credit by talking to people in the industry.
What does the assessment involve?	Poster and fact sheet. We need to check: format of the poster (size etc.); how long we will be asked questions; any format requirements for the fact sheet.
How should we organise our answers?	Our poster will look at website development in three areas – business and commerce, education, and entertainment – and then present some general conclusions. Our fact sheet will include examples and weblinks.
What are the assessment criteria?	Tutor checklist includes: quality of research; argument; and quality of the presentation.

Key question	Your response
What will the tutor think is a 'good' project?	The assignment asks us to: produce accurate information which shows that we have done the necessary research; produce conclusions we can back up; and present poster and fact sheet. The poster and fact sheet must summarise our main argument and contain the most important information. They must be well presented and easy to understand. We must be ready to answer questions on the poster.
What sort of 'audience' will the tutors be?	Tutors will be asking us questions about the poster and fact sheet. They will be in their tutor role and so we can use technical terms and assume they know how the technology works.

See the 'Making Groupwork Work' website (listed in 'Useful resources') for more detailed examples.

Examples

Groups of first-year Social Science students had to find an important and recent study of group behaviour *and* explain how its findings related to their own experience of coming to university. Several groups found interesting studies and did lots of background reading but their presentations did not explicitly consider how the work related to their own experience –they failed to address one of the main assessment criteria. As a result, their presentations were graded lower than those groups who had read the assessment brief more carefully.

Groups of first-year Media students were asked to edit a short podcast from the tutor which included many errors (pauses, slips of the tongue, 'ums' etc.). All the groups except one edited out the errors. One group did more complicated edits, which made the tutor's speech much worse (and very funny). Their accompanying notes showed clearly how their edits met the assessment criteria (critical analysis, applying principles) – and received top marks. So you can be successful by thinking creatively about the task – but make sure you have the confidence and detailed preparation to carry it off.

Generating ideas

Once everyone is clear about the task, the group can start discussing ideas about how to proceed. How do we find out people's initial thoughts?

There are a number of ways of doing this. For example:

▸ do an organised brainstorm
▸ use 'sticky notes' so individuals can jot down individual suggestions and you can stick them on the board
▸ use 'concept mapping' or ideas mapping software to generate ideas.

An example of a concept map listing some of or the first ideas for Task A (using free software – CMAP) is on the next page. These initial thoughts can then be turned into an overall plan.

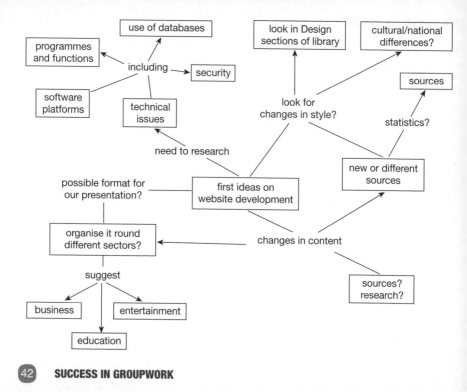

Making your plan

A good plan does not have to be a very complicated document. It does need to be agreed and shared, though, and it does need to have clear targets and deadlines.

Milestones

When working on a group project, you need to identify the key targets that have to be achieved at particular stages – these are often called 'milestones'. They determine how you need to organise your time. When you plan your milestones, you should start from the final deadline and work back. Look at the example outline plan for a group doing Task A on the next page.

Example project plan for Task A

Wk	Need to do	Project milestones
1	*Meeting 1* Make introductions and agree ground rules Share initial ideas on project Agree who will do initial research	Share contact information Agree ground rules
2	*Meeting 2* Agree topic – websites Agree how to approach it (areas to investigate) Allocate individuals to areas	Agree on topic and approach Delegate members to specific areas to research
3	*Meeting 3* Discuss research so far Decide what further research is necessary	
4	*Meeting 4* Compare results of research in three areas Discuss overall format of presentation Decide on extra materials (handouts)	Complete research Decide on conclusions Agree format of presentation
5	*Meeting 5* Report progress on sections and handouts Review action plan	

Wk	Need to do	Project milestones
6	*Meetings 6 & 7* Compile material into final presentation + handouts Final rehearsal of the presentation.	Agree and rehearse final presentation

Before you finalise your plan, do a reality check.

For example, this plan leaves only 2 weeks to do the research – is this enough? What if you decide to contact some people in organisations to talk to – are you confident that you will be able to find the right contact and arrange a meeting at such short notice?

Have you given yourself enough time to rehearse and polish the presentation?

Can you give everyone a fair share of the workload? For example, if you have five members and three areas to research, how do you allocate tasks?

Reality checklist

	OK?
Does this timescale fit in with group members' existing commitments? Will everyone be able to get to all the meetings?	
Does this plan give you the basis for a fair distribution of workload?	
Are your timescales realistic? Allow extra time to take account of slippage, delays, and the unexpected …	

8   Team roles

Some groups decide that the best way to organise themselves is to allocate certain roles. Team roles often include a leader/manager – but beware adopting styles which will only work in an organisation with a clear hierarchy (see the next theory box).

Other roles which student groups often develop include note-taker/secretary, researcher, designer, etc. Having set roles can make it easier to allocate tasks but it can also be a source of conflict, as some roles are perceived to have more responsibility or volume of work than others.

Theory box: Leadership vs. management

Theory

Some theorists have distinguished between 'leadership' skills (making sure the group is going in a clear direction, especially in change situations) and 'management' skills (making sure the group is well organised and productive – the preferred style for situations of 'stability'). Being a leader or manager was seen as mutually exclusive: you were either one or the other. More recent research (Quinn 2000) has found that a good balance of all of these skills is required to lead effective teams. Effective leaders must be able to manage and effective managers must be able to lead – they need to deploy different styles at different times to ensure continued team success.

Comment

Most research on leadership and management has looked at groups in organisations, not in education. In student groups, it may be useful to consider a team leader/manager as more of a 'facilitator' rather than someone who gives orders or instructions. She or he has to use their persuasive skills to ensure good communication, organised and fair working, and a positive team climate.

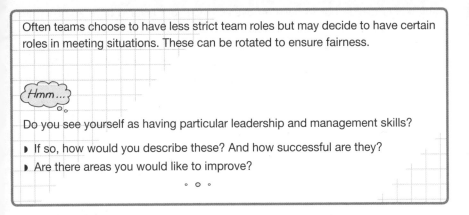

Often teams choose to have less strict team roles but may decide to have certain roles in meeting situations. These can be rotated to ensure fairness.

Hmm...

Do you see yourself as having particular leadership and management skills?

▶ If so, how would you describe these? And how successful are they?
▶ Are there areas you would like to improve?

∘ ○ ∘

Deciding group roles

Good leadership can help keep a group focused and motivated and ensure that things move forward by deciding things quickly. This does not mean that one person has to 'be leader'. Groups can organise themselves in different ways and be equally effective. You need to decide on a way of working which suits your mix of personalities and also gets the job done. That is why it is useful for the group to discuss how you are going to do things.

Many teams decide not to have an overall leader but instead have someone lead or 'chair' the team meetings. This role can then be rotated or shared to ensure that more than one team member gets the chance to do this and that the responsibility is shared. You can also decide to rotate or share the roles in the following table – this allows members to develop different skills. Rotation also helps since some of these roles are more popular than others.

Group roles

Role	Description
Facilitator/chair	Directs the discussion and attempts to ensure that the meeting is productive.
Secretary/note-taker	Makes notes of the key discussion points and meeting decisions.
Timekeeper	Ensures that the team is aware of the time and keeps the conversation moving if the team spends too long on a topic.
Task manager	Records the team actions, and who is supposed to do them and when they need to be done by. Records contact between meetings. Prepares agenda for next meeting.

Another way of deciding on the roles and organisation you need is to look at some of the theories on roles which social scientists have developed, and we give an example in the following theory box.

Theory box: Team roles

Theory

One of the most popular theories of team roles is the model developed by Meredith Belbin on the basis of his research and observations of management teams (Belbin 2010). Based on ideas of intrinsic personality traits, Belbin devised a self-diagnostic tool to assess the roles that an individual is most likely to adopt when working in a group.

His model defines nine roles which all make a positive contribution to an effective team (earlier versions of the book suggested the first eight of these, which are probably the most important for student groups).

Belbin's team roles

Role	Someone who is effective in this role will be good at ...
Implementer	getting things done and focusing on practical issues
Coordinator	organising the task and the other members of the group
Shaper	inspiring and leading the group from the front
Plant	generating ideas and being creative
Resource investigator	identifying resources that can help, which may be outside the group
Monitor/evaluator	evaluating ideas and proposals and pointing out possible flaws
Team worker	getting everyone to cooperate and work together
Completer/finisher	working to deadlines and getting jobs completed
Specialist	providing specialist technical expertise

Belbin's model identifies all the positive behaviours which an effective group needs. He also identified 'allowable weaknesses' for each role – if you are good at this, then it's OK to be not so good at that. He included a self-test version of his questionnaire in earlier editions of the book which many students have completed.

Some courses now use his full and updated commercial version to establish project groups so as to provide a good spread of roles in each group.

Comment

No group of four or five students will have all the roles represented by different individuals! Each person will have a couple of strong roles and some roles that are not so strong or not preferred ways of behaving. Belbin himself argued that a group could adjust its behaviour if it discovered that it had a balance of roles that was not ideal. For example, he describes a group of strong Shapers who were not making progress because everyone wanted to lead. The group agreed on a set of rules and procedures which enabled them to work together.

While Belbin's model offers a useful starting point, it cannot be accepted as the last word in group analysis. Some recent studies (Partington and Harris 1999; Aritzeta et al. 2007) have found that teams do not seem to benefit from, nor need a good balance of, these roles to succeed.

Hmm...

Think of your own group experience and consider how the different members acted in more or less predictable ways.

▶ Have you noticed that certain people tend to take certain roles?
▶ What were these roles?
▶ To what extent do you think Belbin-type theory can be useful?

∘ O ∘

You can also use Belbin's roles as a checklist of things which need to happen in your group, e.g. is the group being coordinated? So you can think about:

▶ Which roles are happening in your group?
▶ Are they all covered?
▶ Are there any gaps? Does it matter? If so, what can you do about it?

Schedule regular meetings. Ideally, try and find a regular time to meet at the start of the project so people can build it in to their schedule (and remember it!)

It can, of course, be difficult to find times to suit everyone and sometimes groups will need to move their meeting times around. If this is the case, make sure everyone knows when the next meeting will be – and remember to contact anyone who didn't make it!

You can discuss this with diaries or use an electronic planner – there are now several free ones available on the web (e.g. www.meetomatic.com/calendar.php).

> **Example**
>
> Top-scoring groups in our management example met regularly outside the class. The most popular time was straight after the class. In the final presentations, you could tell which groups had met more often as they were much better prepared and clearly knew each other quite well!

Agendas

An agenda sets out what you hope to discuss in a meeting. Ideally, one person (note-taker? task manager?) will have prepared an outline before the meeting. At the beginning of the meeting, ask everyone if they want to add items to it.

Good agendas make sure that you can discuss and record:
- progress on the project
- what needs to be done next
- any problems that need to be resolved.

The meeting should cover all the items on your agenda. If you run out of time, it is good practice to add the agenda item you didn't get to discuss to the agenda of the next meeting, or decide on an extra meeting to resolve the outstanding issue.

It is essential that at the end of the meeting everyone is clear about when the next meeting is and when their actions need to be completed by. If possible, details of this should be sent to everyone (e.g. by email or posted to a wiki). Make sure that everyone understands what needs to be done.

Sample agenda

The example that follows shows how you can organise your discussion to cover the ideas discussed above. Using a table format gives you space to record decisions and make notes – remember to be very clear on who is doing what (and by when). You could also use separate columns for notes and decisions/actions.

Sample agenda

Project meeting agenda Library meeting room 2 10am–11am Wednesday 23 November		
	Item	*Notes and decisions/actions*
1	Welcome and introductions	
2	Apologies	
3	Purpose of meeting	
4	Progress on agreed actions	

Project meeting agenda Library meeting room 2 10am–11am Wednesday 23 November	
Item	*Notes and decisions/actions*
4.1. Jack to report on poster costs	
4.2 Zahara to update on design contact	
4.3 Asif to present data findings	
5 Workload review	
6 Planning for presentation	
6.1 Presentation idea (Zahara)	
6.2 Materials for poster (Jack)	
7 Mike's absence	
8 Any other business	
9 Actions: who does what by the next meeting	
10 Time and date of next meeting	

Spreading the load

What do you do if some tasks or sections are more heavyweight than others? There are various things you can do to monitor this – ask members to keep a rough guide of the time they are spending on particular tasks. Also, suggest time limits when you divide up tasks and allocate them.

Contingency/back-up

What will you do if someone is ill? When you are allocating tasks, it can be a good idea to nominate a back-up person for each task just in case illness or some other factor prevents that person from completing their task. Working out which tasks are essential and which are optional extras can also help you decide which to forget about in the event of a crisis.

Example

The Business group agreed that three people would each come up with the content for a skill that they would be talking about in the presentation. However, since there were more than three people in the group, what were the others going to do? One was really shy and nervous about presenting. The group decided that this person would design the introduction and conclusion slides and that the others would talk to one of these slides in the presentation. The shy member also had to send whatever notes they had on the three skills to the other members to help them design their slide content. They agreed that this seemed fair.

And someone who doesn't pull their weight?

One group member didn't show up to many of the meetings and didn't do what he said he was going to. The other group members divided the work up between them and made sure that they mentioned this in their written reflections/peer assessment task.

Your group should have discussed in the first meeting how you want decisions made. After a couple of meetings, review how this is working.

I vote we aim for consensus!

Deciding methods

Deciding method	Pros	Cons
Consensus	Everyone is committed to the decision and feels a part of it.	Can take more time. May need a chairperson who is good at managing discussion.
Compromise	Gets the group to a decision.	Does not always resolve underlying issues. May lead to conflict later.

Deciding method	Pros	Cons
Leader/chair decides	Simple, often quick.	Possible team resentment, risk of poor choice and limited group responsibility.
Vote	Usually considered fair, efficient in 'non-even' groups.	Can lead to a split group if there is an equal number on each side. May give problems if there are strong minority opinions.
Pros/cons table	Efficient and can help to clarify a difficult and complicated decision.	Can be time-consuming and choices may still appear quite closely matched.
Random selection	Quick, allows groups to move forward where other methods have failed.	Can result in poor/ ill-informed choices.

Example

Our Business group chose to do their presentation on interpersonal skills because the members of that group felt they knew more about these than intrapersonal skills. As no one had very strong feelings, they voted. Choosing which interpersonal skills to do was a bit trickier. At first they tried to choose the skills as a group but couldn't agree on a top three. Eventually, they decided that three people would present a skill each and each could choose which skill to use.

Takeaway tips

▶ Organise your meetings well.
▶ Be clear on the task.
▶ Break the task down into manageable bits.
▶ Create a plan which everyone can see and understand.
▶ Decide (and keep under review) how you are making decisions.
▶ Be realistic and think about contingency.

PART 4

RELATIONSHIPS AND COMMUNICATION

This part outlines strategies for keeping your group on track in terms of your relationships and communication. It includes:

- analysing what is going on
- reviewing and revising your ground rules
- dealing with conflict.

Entertainers talk about 'reading' their audience – studying their actions and reactions to decide how they are likely to respond (and adjusting their act accordingly). You can develop skills in 'reading' your group – deciding what is going on and how people are feeling and then determining what you can or should do about it.

Don't we all do this already?

Yes, we all do to some extent. But sometimes groups do not recognise what is going on and sometimes members misinterpret each other.

Example: the 'democratic' group with the dominant leader

The tutor asked the group how they were getting on. All the members looked at Sally. She immediately responded, saying how well they were doing and how they had decided to 'be democratic with no one leading'. And the other members all nodded. This happened every time the tutor asked for comment or a decision. The group got stuck later – they did not recognise they were leaving Sally to work out and decide everything. And then she ran out of energy and inspiration …

Interpreting your group's behaviour

There are various ways of analysing how groups communicate, many based on formal techniques used by social scientists – see the theory box on page 72 for a brief introduction.

The following techniques are designed to help you reflect, to help you as an individual gain an insight into what is going on. They are not intended as activities for you to introduce to the group; they simply offer an extra dimension to your understanding and reflection about how your group is working.

Some tutors use exercises like these in group discussion. They can be very effective but only if the tutor is skilled and experienced and there is plenty of time. People can develop strong feelings in their group and so discussion needs to be carefully managed.

Interaction chart

This is a simple diagram of communication between the group members. It is an 'ideal' group where everyone is communicating positively and equally with everyone else.

You are unlikely to find such a group in real life. There will always be some imbalance.

How would you like to be a member of the following group?

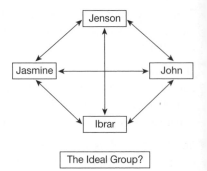

The Ideal Group?

In this example, Duane sends and receives messages from everyone and will probably be seen as the leader. Jo, Aaron and Stella seem to be a bit of a subgroup and Hans seems to be rather isolated. To improve relationships in this group, individuals need to take responsibility in different ways:

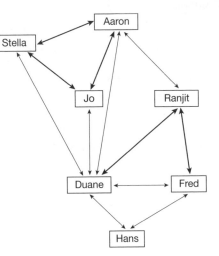

- Duane needs to recognise how central he is and try to get everyone equally involved.

- Jo, Aaron and Stella need to see how their friendship is excluding others.

- Hans needs to consider why he is on the edge of the group. Has he given the impression that he is uninterested or unwilling to join in? Or have the others ignored him because he is a bit shy?

Analogy

Sometimes it is easier to use an analogy or visual image to express an idea. What is your group like? Would you describe it as a jaguar (the animal) – sleek, fast, flexible and fit, but not necessarily very friendly? Or is it more of a teddy bear – warm and cuddly but a bit slow to do anything? A 'jaguar' group may need to spend more time working on relationships; a 'teddy bear' group may need to adopt a more urgent approach to the task.

Boundaries and participation

Another approach is to think about the group boundaries. Who is central to the group and who is on the edge? You may decide that there is a boundary within the group so that really there are two subgroups in the room. This can be a problem – the subgroups may develop a different approach to the group task (see the next theory box).

Example of boundary problems

Discussion in this group felt like a table tennis match, with the ball being a comment or idea and the two players being the younger students and the older ones who had taken seats at opposite sides of the table. From individual discussion, the tutor discovered that each subgroup had developed a positive image of itself and a negative image of the others. The younger students felt intimidated by the older students' confidence. The older students felt intimidated by the younger students' better grasp of academic work. The atmosphere only improved when the tutor introduced ideas and theories of group conflict into their discussion.

Theory box: Observing group behaviour

Theory

Social scientists have used a wide range of techniques and approaches to observe group behaviour (see Hogg and Vaughan 2008). One approach has used external observers to categorise and record individual behaviours and see what patterns emerge over time. Research studies have also used methods such as participant observation to gain more subjective views from group members. Studies have looked at circumstances where groups see themselves in conflict with another group (what is often called 'intergroup behaviour') and found that conflict can be very quick to develop and unfortunately take a lot of time and energy to resolve.

Comment

Different methods give you different views of what is happening, so there is no one best way which suits all situations. Questionnaire and survey tools are available for things like group climate (atmosphere) or openness to innovation.

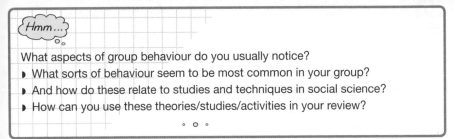

Hmm...

What aspects of group behaviour do you usually notice?

▶ What sorts of behaviour seem to be most common in your group?

▶ And how do these relate to studies and techniques in social science?

▶ How can you use these theories/studies/activities in your review?

° O °

Can't hear you!

whirr

Clank

What?

12 Reviewing and revising your ground rules

In Part 2 we discussed ground rules in two categories:

▶ communication and attitudes
▶ working practice.

Agreeing rules does not mean that they will automatically work. Review them at least once – ideally at the halfway point in time in a project. This should give you time to change and improve if you need to.

Make sure your ground rules are still useful and relevant.

One good way to do this is to turn each of your rules into a question – are we doing 'X'? (where X is the original ground rule). If the answer is no, then what is the consequence? Does this matter? If it does and it is getting in the way of group progress, then you need to renew or revise the ground rule. The rest of this section demonstrates how to approach this.

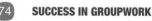

Communication and attitudes

Virtually everyone wants their team to treat everyone with respect and dignity. You can translate this into a personal checklist as below. You can also ask all the group members to complete it. If the answer is 'no' to any of the questions, then you need to change – or relationships and communication will go downhill. See the corresponding section for advice.

Ground rules checklist

Original ground rules (see p. 28)	In practice by ...	See section below ...
Use positive body language	Am I projecting myself positively through body language? Am I interpreting other members' body language correctly?	A
Give everyone a chance to speak	Do I allow time for people to speak and respond to key points?	B
Listen and pay attention to each other	Do I ask people for their opinions and thoughts? Do I actively listen to what others have to say?	C

Original ground rules (see p. 28)	In practice by ...	See section below ...
Acknowledge other members' opinions	Do I acknowledge and consider others' ideas and thoughts in a reasonable and balanced way?	D

A – Body language

Is your body language positive and encouraging? And are you interpreting others' body language correctly?

Body language is a complex issue with many cultural variations, so when you consider the body language of other group members do not be dogmatic about what it means. Rather than looking for particular signals (like someone crossing their arms, which supposedly suggests they are being defensive), look for any *changes* in a person's typical body language. If someone regularly uses a lot of gestures and hand movements when they talk then notice if they are doing this more or less than normal. Changes like this can give clues to the person's feelings.

That said, there are some general tips that may help. If you find someone seems to be getting annoyed at you for any reason, check your body language. You may be sending out the wrong signals!

Do ...	Try not to ...
Face the person you are talking to	Fidget, fiddle with your mobile etc.
Use eye contact (but be aware that some people are unused to this, and culture plays a part here)	Flop about, looking disconnected

B – Giving everyone a chance to speak

All group members should be given time to speak and contribute, especially in response to a major idea or decision.

In any group there will be confident people and those that are less so. There is always a danger that groups will be dominated, especially in discussion, by strong characters and that shy or nervous members will be ignored or not given enough of an opportunity to voice their thoughts and ideas.

If you are a confident person, try to encourage other people to get involved wherever possible. Sometimes they have good ideas but are just too shy to say them. From the other perspective, if you are shy and someone asks for your opinion, try to say what you think – they want to know! It can help to write some thoughts down first so you know what you want to say.

Try:
- allowing 'thinking time' or silence so people can think about the key points
- agreeing a limit for how long one person can talk for
- taking it in turns to speak in a set order (e.g. clockwise round a circle)
- asking people what they think in order to encourage participation.

C – Active listening

People often concentrate on what they are going to say next, rather than pay attention to what someone else is saying right now. To be an active listener you need to:

▶ understand the message being passed to you, and
▶ communicate that you have received and understood the message.

Taking brief notes by writing key words can help if someone has a lot to say. You can then check your understanding by rephrasing and repeating back what they have said or you could ask a question to clarify a key point. Remember your body language!

Try:

▶ summarising what the other person has said in your own words:
  D *So, what you are saying is …*
  D *Ok, so you think that …*
  D *Right, you are suggesting that we …*
▶ encouraging the other person non-verbally:
  D nod occasionally
  D make some eye contact
  D ensure that you are facing them.

For visual/multimedia examples, see www.learnhigher.ac.uk. Or search for 'active listening' on www.youtube.com.

D – Acknowledging others

Communication is a two-way process. You, of course, want to get your message across effectively, but you also need to listen to and understand what other people are trying to tell you.

Sometimes you can get things wrong. So you do need to listen to what other people have to say – even if they express it in a way that seems to you to be rude or disrespectful. If someone has upset you, let them know – they may have done it without realising. You also need to make sure that you don't miss the useful part of the message.

At times, it can seem easier to say nothing but if you spot something that the other group members haven't, by discussing it as a group you might solve a looming problem and save yourself from a greater challenge later. It is better to raise your concerns and be proved wrong than to remain silent and be proved right.

Likewise, when you raise a point of view, explain it clearly. It is easy to say that you don't like an idea. It is more useful, however, to say why. In the following example, a student wants to suggest that an idea will prove difficult due to its being too time consuming. Compare different ways of expressing this view.

You say …	Is this the best way to say it?
I don't like your idea.	No, this is a value judgement and is personal.
I'm not sure about that idea.	Better, not personal but a bit vague.
That's one way we could do it, but I think it might be too time consuming.	Much better. This acknowledges the previous contribution but raises a valid point in a non-personal way.
That's one way we could do it, which would work, but I wonder if it might be too time consuming. Could we try this instead?	Very good. This acknowledges the previous idea, clearly states your opinion and suggests a possible alternative. It is even more likely to be seen as constructive if your suggestion obviously develops or builds on the other person's proposal.

These suggestions will help you to get away from 'yes, but' thinking where we immediately think of what might be wrong with someone's suggestion.

Working practice

Is your team making good progress on the task? Revisit your ground rules on this to see if you can identify any areas for improvement.

Keeping in contact

People are busy and will sometimes have to miss meetings – work, family and the unexpected can mean finding a regular time everyone can make really difficult. But do try and establish ways of staying in touch between meetings.

In between meetings, you might have decided to keep in touch via email/mobile/online communication. Is this working?

What rules did you establish at the start? Are these rules being maintained? Do they need re-emphasising or renewing?

Can you use technology to help? Would social networking software like Facebook work for everyone? Is there a similar space offered by your course? Most college and university courses now have online spaces – check whether this includes a discussion space for your group.

Working practice checklist

If the answer is 'no' for any of these questions it is probably the group organisation you need to improve (see Part 3 for advice).

Working practice checklist

Original ground rules	Key questions	OK?	If not, go back to this section in Part 3 ...
When and where will the team meet?	Are team meetings efficient and organised?		Agendas
Behave professionally	Is everyone turning up for meetings? Does everyone communicate if they are delayed or can't make it? Is everyone doing what they agreed to?		Organising meetings
Will there be team or meeting roles?	If you have team roles, are they working well? If you don't have team roles, do you need them?		Team roles

Original ground rules	Key questions	OK?	If not, go back to this section in Part 3 …
How will we decide things?	Is your team deciding things effectively? Do you need to change your deciding method?		Making decisions

13 Dealing with conflict

Sometimes, for a variety of reasons, a group will find itself in conflict. This can upset everyone and may have a severe impact on effective group working. What can you do if this happens to your group?

Managing and resolving conflict

When conflict does arise, consider the following four key steps.

1 Open the lines of communication

Professional mediators usually insist on what they call the 'conflict-resolving conversation'. They know the value of making each party sit down around a table and discuss how they might move forward. You need a meeting which *everyone* attends.

2 Define the issues

Do the opposing parties have the same idea about what the issues actually are? Or do they see things very differently?

Try this:

▶ Each person writes down on sticky notes why there is disagreement (one note for each separate comment).

▶ Sticky notes are put on the board or table and the group discussion sorts them into issues to resolve.

Consider: Is it a task-based issue, perhaps a difference of opinion about the best course of action? Or is it a person-centred issue, perhaps a problem relating to reliability or commitment? Can the group continue the project or does this issue need to be resolved before you proceed?

3 Focus on the task

When issues relate to personality clashes or personal difference, people tend to focus more on the issue and less on the task. The technique above should start the group thinking about how to get on with the task. You need to reinforce this in the discussion – if it looks as if personal differences are getting in the way, ask a question or make a comment which will refocus on the task, such as, *We disagree on this but how can we move forward?* Everyone in the group should try to do this.

4 Use your group ground rules

Group conflicts often arise from disagreements about how a group should proceed when several options are on the table. You should have committed to certain ways of deciding things in your original ground rules. Go back to the rules and review them again. If you are still stuck or can't work things out, seek help from your tutor.

Conflict resolution is a major area of international research and study. There are plenty of websites with tips on how to resolve group conflict. See if you can find any that might help you reflect on your own situation and add further tips to the ones above.

∘ O ∘

Examples

The design students who could not agree

The course contained a week-long practical group project. One group came to a tutor in the middle of the week, minus one member, saying they had reached an impasse. The missing member, Jay, had a completely different approach to the design and was not willing to budge. The tutor explained that this was not uncommon in design consultancy work and the group would have to figure out a way of resolving the disagreement or using it constructively in their final presentation. The group went back to Jay and decided to adopt this second suggestion. In their final presentation, they discussed both the majority and minority view. The other tutors on the judging panel (who were completely unaware of the conflict) decided that this was one of the best and most thoughtful presentations. All the members of the group, including Jay, were extremely satisfied with both the process and the outcome.

The business students with the missing member

The group struggled to get any responses from one group member. They could not get him to turn up to meetings so they could have a discussion. Finally, they mentioned this to their tutor. He advised them to continue working together without the missing member; to keep a clear record of attendance and contribution; and have a plan about what they might allow him to do if he decided to get back in touch (perhaps contribute some slides or do a bit of the presentation). The tutor reminded them that it would be clear from the individual assignment who had not contributed to their group and that there were marks from peer assessment. This demonstrates that you need a back-up plan if conflict resolution fails.

See 'Making Groupwork Work', Episode 6, www.learnhighergroupwork.com.

Think about any conflicts you have been involved in in the past that you managed to solve.

▶ How did you resolve the conflict?
▶ Do you think you were able to think rationally at the time?

What did you learn from the experience?

 **Takeaway tips**

▶ Develop your observation skills to identify what is happening in the group.
▶ Review your ground rules and make sure that they continue to support positive communication and constructive debate.
▶ If conflict emerges, deal with it by focusing on the issues and working through them.

ASSESSMENT AND REFLECTION

This part will help you to:

- check that you have met the demands of the current assignment
- reflect upon your experience of groupwork
- write this reflection up for an assignment
- use this experience to do things better next time.

The final section of this book is a troubleshooting guide which summarises main ideas covered in this book.

Meeting assessment criteria

On pages 35–7 we emphasised the importance of working out in detail what the assignment was about. What counts as good performance? This is a really important point and we make no apology for repeating it.

Time spent analysing assessment details and criteria will really pay off. Below we consider the group presentation, where many group projects finish. You can, however, apply similar questions to whatever 'product' your project has to deliver.

Delivering an effective presentation

Your tutor will provide instructions for the presentation. Use the following checklist to make sure that you have all the necessary information. The notes in italics suggest issues you need to sort out.

Presentation checklist

Key question	Notes
Where will the presentation take place?	*Make sure you visit this room beforehand and get to know it. Ideally, try to book it for a rehearsal.*
How long do we have?	*Make sure you keep to time. Many tutors will cut you off at the allotted time regardless of whether you have finished.*
What facilities will we have? What is the expected format?	*Use of PowerPoint is now fairly standard but what about alternatives? And what if the tutor excludes PowerPoint? Are you expected to produce a handout?*
Who is the audience?	*Will your tutor be listening and questioning from a particular perspective or role? Will other student groups or other people be there?*
What is its purpose?	*For example, are you being asked to summarise all the work you have done or just present the conclusions and implications? Do you have to relate what you have done to work elsewhere (perhaps major theories or industrial practice?)*
What is the best way of achieving this?	*Is a conventional PowerPoint presentation the best way to put across your message?*
Who has to present?	*Does everyone have to take a turn and say a bit? If not, how are you going to organise the group while the presentation is going on?*

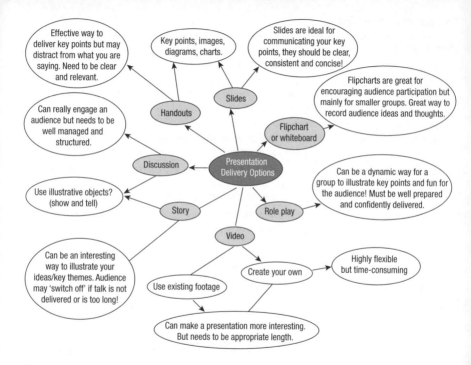

Effective way to deliver key points but may distract from what you are saying. Need to be clear and relevant.

Key points, images, diagrams, charts.

Slides are ideal for communicating your key points, they should be clear, consistent and concise!

Flipcharts are great for encouraging audience participation but mainly for smaller groups. Great way to record audience ideas and thoughts.

Can really engage an audience but needs to be well managed and structured.

Handouts

Slides

Flipchart or whiteboard

Presentation Delivery Options

Discussion

Story

Role play

Video

Can be a dynamic way for a group to illustrate key points and fun for the audience! Must be well prepared and confidently delivered.

Use illustrative objects? (show and tell)

Can be an interesting way to illustrate your ideas/key themes. Audience may 'switch off' if talk is not delivered or is too long!

Create your own

Use existing footage

Highly flexible but time-consuming

Can make a presentation more interesting. But needs to be appropriate length.

Examples

The Business students with a varied presentation

In their presentation they used:

- PowerPoint for key points
- video recording of the group performing a role play
- brief practical exercise for everyone
- questions to the audience.

The presentation was well received. They made their key points and the presentation was well rehearsed.

One problem did emerge – the non-participating member showed up (which annoyed other group members) and even stood with the group when they presented. As his name was not on the introduction slide and he wasn't in the video, it was obvious that he had not contributed very much. This led to his poor mark, based on the group's peer assessment by other group members and the tutor's mark.

The other Business students who flunked the game

The course included a business game. By making regular decisions to build a profitable business, student groups had to 'beat' the computer simulation and make better decisions than the other groups.

One group made a couple of bad decisions and realised they had virtually no chance of winning the game. They then concentrated on working out the assumptions on which the game is based. They reasoned that this would give them a head start on the written assignment. After the game was finished, it was clear that this group understood the business game (and met the assessment criteria) better than the group who actually won. This was reflected in good marks in the subsequent assignment.

By reflecting upon what they really needed to learn, this group turned the business game into effective preparation for their assessment.

15 Reflecting on your experience

What makes 'good' reflection?

The point about feedback is to use it – to help you to review your performance and plan to improve upon it next time. Reflection can be a powerful tool for learning from experience and doing differently – and better – next time.

Being open to feedback

Accepting the need to improve is not always easy. The first step in using feedback is recognising that feedback is a vital and useful part of self-development and we can only use it fully if we are open to the information.

Do you need more information?

To use feedback – whether from tutors or other students – you need to understand it. If feedback is not completely clear, contact the person who provided the feedback and seek clarification. You can only reflect on information that you understand and it is perfectly reasonable to ask for more if you need it.

Five-step reflection model

Many students are confused by what tutors want from a reflection. You will be able to satisfy most tutors if you can answer the following five questions:

What did you and the group do well?

The first stage is to recognise the aspects of your work that you completed well. This should include anything you know went well or you have received praise for. Make sure you understand why it was viewed positively.

How did you feel about what happened?

Don't ignore any feelings you might have, as these are important clues.

What could be improved?

The next stage involves identifying comments from any feedback that indicate that there is room for improvement.

How can you explain what worked and what did not?

Most tutors will not be satisfied if you just describe what happened in your group. They want you to relate your experience to general principles and theory to show that you have deepened your understanding of group process.

How would you do things differently next time?

The final part of reflection involves identifying possible actions you can take to improve your performance next time.

The theory boxes in this book offer you some start points (and references to follow up) for exploring some of the groupwork theory you may choose to draw on in your reflective analysis. You may see the connections between a particular theory and your experience in your group – or you may not. Either way, this comparison between how your group worked and a particular theory will give your work that analytical dimension.

The following template gives you a structure for recording an event or situation that you want to reflect on – an example is in italics.

Reflection template

Event (include date and time)	*14 November, 2.00–3.30* *Meeting to try out the presentation for the first time*
What happened?	*We all arrived on time except for Jed who arrived at 2.15. We did not start till after he arrived.* *We did two run-throughs of the presentation with all the PowerPoint slides and then had a discussion of each to see where we could improve.* *We changed a few of the slides for the second run-through.* *We agreed to meet before the final formal presentation to have a final run-through.*

Event (include date and time)	14 November, 2.00–3.30
	Meeting to try out the presentation for the first time
How did you feel?	I felt frustrated that we started late; it did not give us enough time to review our first run-through as thoroughly as I would have liked.
What went well?	Our overall argument came across much better in the second run-through.
What could be improved?	Jed arriving late created some tension as he did not offer any explanation.
	Our timing is still a bit wrong as we are still 2 minutes over.
How can you explain what worked and what did not?	We do not seem to have developed into a well-organised team if you look at the theories on 'effective teams'. We seem to have accepted Jed as leader because of his level of self-confidence but he does not seem to want to live up to our expectations.
What have I learnt and what would I do differently next time?	We did not have a contingency plan for anyone arriving late – what if this happened on the day?

If you have made notes on important events in your group's history, you will have plenty of material to use in your write-up when you draw on some of the theory introduced in this book (see Kolb, p. 6, Belbin, pp. 52–4 or the five steps, p. 98).

There are two things that can help you decide what should go into the assignment:

▶ What are the issues or themes that have cropped up on a few occasions?
(In the example above, there are likely to be regular issues of coordination and leadership.)

▶ What comparisons can you make between your experience of the group and generally accepted ideas and theories about group behaviour?

The next theory box gives you one example of such comparisons.

Theory box: Models of group development

Theory

Perhaps the best-known theory with regard to group development was devised by Bruce Tuckman (see in Hartley 1997), based on a review of previous studies. His four stages are often cited as the definitive model.

Tuckman suggested that most groups go through a series of recognisable stages during the course of a project. These are:

Forming There is uncertainty and insecurity, as group members get to know one another and work out how they might work together.

Storming Conflict and disagreement surface as group members become more confident and comfortable in airing their opinions. Power struggles and cliques may develop.

Norming Consensus emerges as the group finds effective ways both to get on with each other and to work together efficiently.

Performing The group becomes effective with a clear, shared view of the task and a settled way of working.

Adjourning (Fifth stage, added later) The group prepares to split up. There can be feelings of satisfaction but also sadness and loss.

Comment

There are a number of alternatives to this model (Hartley 1997, 2005).

You should always try to identify limitations in the theories you look at. For example, Tuckman based his model on a survey of studies of groups which he could find at the time, back in the 1960s and 1970s. Modern project groups have a wide range of tools at their disposal which may enable them to work differently, e.g. the enhanced communication offered through mobile phones and the ability to share information across the internet.

Although Tuckman's model may not apply universally, it can serve as a useful tool in highlighting common scenarios that groups face to students embarking on a group project.

> *Hmm...*

Tuckman offers a useful model for looking back at the whole process.

How far did your group follow this pattern?

Don't worry if your group didn't follow this pattern! One student group apologised in a tutorial that they 'didn't seem to be doing it right as they had not stormed'. The tutor had to explain that this is only one model of how groups behave. If you got on well, sorted out the task efficiently, completed the assignment well and positively, and are still getting on fine ... you will not have followed the pattern Tuckman describes. Can you explain how and why you did this? This group avoided storming by being very well organised and cooperative, and were able to say how they did it.

∘ O ∘

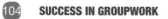

Action planning

On the basis of the feedback you get from tutors, you should also be able to set targets to improve next time. Try to phrase your targets in ways that make them easier to achieve – set targets which are specific, measurable, achievable, realistic and with a clear time schedule.

A good target will have clear deadlines for specific action. So, if your tutor said you gave an 'overlong and woolly' introduction to your last presentation, you could turn this into targets for next time.

Targets checklist

	Check ✔
Is my target/goal specific enough?	*Target is to get good feedback on my next introduction*
Is my goal measurable?	*Will ask tutor for specific measure*
Is my goal achievable?	*Yes*

	Check ✔
Is my goal realistic?	*I need to improve my style. I will research ideas on good presentations over the next 4 weeks, and volunteer to do the introduction on our next presentation.*
Is my goal time-bound (have I set a date it needs to be completed by)?	*Next presentation is in 4 weeks*

And a final Hmm …

Think about your experience of groupwork and what you have learnt.

▶ What did you do well?
▶ What could you have improved?
▶ What have you learnt from the experience and/or this book?
▶ What might you do differently next time you are in a group?

○ ○ ○

 **Takeaway tips**

- Revisit the assessment brief and criteria regularly and check you have satisfied them.
- Be open to feedback and reflection.
- Know what you did well and look for explanations.
- Know what could be improved.
- Record your thoughts regularly if you have to write a reflective assignment.
- Set some targets for development.

Troubleshooting guide

Issue	Suggested solution
Don't know where to start	• Start with introductions and maybe a discussion of group members' skills/interests. • Discuss and decide on your ground rules. • Get everyone to read a copy of the assignment instructions and the marking criteria if you have it. Give everyone 5 minutes to come up with initial thoughts – share with group. • Discuss together and record ideas/thoughts somewhere!
Don't know how to get organised	• Meet regularly! • Create a plan. • Decide on your final product/output. Work backwards from the hand-in date and think of all the stages you need to complete and how long you would need for each. • Break the plan into 'mini-tasks' and allocate these to group members with targets for completion. • Record who is doing what. • Discuss your plan and progress in your meetings.

Issue	Suggested solution
Can't decide what to do	• Write all your options down. • Draw up a list of pros and cons. • Choose top two options. • Take a vote on best option. • If this doesn't work, choose by random selection. • Move on.
Group conflict	• Get each group member to write down what they think the problem is. Put the comments up for everyone to read and get the group to discuss the priorities. • Get the group to sit down together and discuss. • Focus on moving forward with the task and on how successful completion will benefit every group member. • Focus on the project actions and ignore any personal differences. What needs to be completed to finish the project? • If all else fails, contact tutor.
Non-participation	• Agree at the start what action you will take if this happens. • Attempt to contact the person and ask them to explain why they are not engaging and what they suggest you do. Explain what will happen if you don't hear from them. • Keep clear records of meetings and attendance and make sure there is a record of who has done what. • Re-allocate any work you need to and complete project without member. • Have a plan for if they re-engage – is there anything you could give them to do? • Inform tutor of your situation as soon as it is obvious there is a problem. • Keep your tutor up to date on how it develops.

References

Aritzeta A, Swailes S, Senior B (2007). Belbin's team role model: development, validity and applications for team building. *Journal of Management Studies* 44(1), pp96–118.

Belbin RM (2010). *Management teams: why they succeed or fail*, 3rd edition. Oxford: Butterworth Heinemann.

Chiocchio F, Essiembre H (2009). Cohesion and performance: a meta-analytic review of disparities between project teams, production teams, and service teams. *Small Group Research* 40(4), pp382–420.

Hartley P (1997). *Group communication*. London: Routledge.

Hartley P (2005). Developing students' skills in groups and teamworking: moving experience into critical reflection. In P Hartley, A Woods and M Pill (eds), *Enhancing teaching in higher education*. London: RoutledgeFalmer.

Harvard Business School (2004). *Teams that click*. Boston: Harvard Business School Press.

Hogg M, Vaughan G (2008). *Social psychology*, 5th edition. Harlow: Prentice Hall.

Kolb DA (1984). *Experiential learning: experience as the source of learning and development.* New Jersey: Prentice Hall.

Partington D, Harris H (1999). Team role balance and team performance: an empirical study. *Journal of Management Development* 18(8), pp694–705.

Quinn RE (2000). *Change the world.* San Francisco: Jossey-Bass.

Seethamraju R, Borman M (2009). Influence of group formation choices on academic performance. *Assessment and Evaluation in Higher Education* 34(1), pp31–40.

Wheelan SA (2009). Group size, group development, and group productivity. *Small Group Research* 40(2), pp247–62.

Useful resources

Weblink for book: **www.palgrave.com/pocketskills/groupwork**
   This website contains further information and weblinks for each part of this book, all the checklists for download, and suggestions on further reading and research.

www.learnhighergroupwork.com/
   'Making Groupwork Work' is the free online resource originally developed by the LearnHigher Centre for Excellence in Teaching and Learning. This is regularly updated with support and advice on working in groups and is organised in episodes that focus on typical group issues. It includes video clips of a particular student group working through a group project and offers advice and links.

You can also find useful links to other resources on the LearnHigher website (**www. learnhigher.ac.uk/**) and the student support site at Bradford (www.bradford.ac.uk/lss/learnerdevelopment/stdev/).

Jacques D, Salmon G (2006). *Learning in groups: a handbook for face-to-face and online environments,* 4th edition. London: Routledge.
   This book has been a major source of inspiration and information for tutors and

students since its first publication in 1984. It now includes useful discussion of online working.

Kahn WA (2009). *The student's guide to successful project teams*. London: Routledge. This contains a more detailed analysis of the issues raised in this book with many useful examples and scenarios of student groups.

West MA (2004). *Effective teamwork: practical lessons from organizational research*. Oxford: Blackwell.
This book contains a lot of useful suggestions based on organisational research into groups.

Index